A

STUDY-SUPPLEMENT

to

KENT'S LECTURES

on

MATERIA MEDICA

A STUDY-SUPPLEMENT *to* KENT'S LECTURES *on* MATERIA MEDICA

(With latest augmentations, commentaries and discussions on various aspects of Homeopathy)

Second Edition

Dr. K.D. KANODIA

B. JAIN PUBLISHERS (P) LTD.
AN ISO 9001 : 2000 CERTIFIED COMPANY

A STUDY-SUPPLEMENT TO KENT'S LECTURES ON MATERIA MEDICA

First Edition: 1993
Second Edition: 2006
3rd Impression: 2020

All rights reserved. No part of this book may be reproduced, stored in a retrieval system or transmitted, in any form or by any means, mechanical, photocopying, recording or otherwise, without any prior written permission of the publisher.

© with the publisher

Published by Kuldeep Jain for
B. JAIN PUBLISHERS (P) LTD.
D-157, Sector-63, NOIDA-201307, U.P. (INDIA)
Tel.: +91-120-4933333 • *Email:* info@bjain.com
Website: **www.bjainbooks.com**
Registered office: 1921/10, Chuna Mandi, Paharganj, New Delhi-110 055 (India)

Printed in India

ISBN: 978-81-319-1398-7

PREFACE TO FIRST EDITION

Homeopathic literature has grown too vast. Many 'pioneers' have contributed to it with their valuable experiences. But there is no parallel to Dr. J.T. Kent (1849-1916). He was a real genius. His works on Philosophy, Materia Medica, and Repertory are not bound to the limits of time. They are for all ages, for all people and for all catagories of readers.

Here is an humble effort to highlight some features of his contributions, and also to present a comparative and analytical study of his materia medica.

Homeopathy today is a developing science, and if the work is helpful to the students and the profession in their deeper studies, I shall feel my efforts rewarded.

Dr. K.D. Kanodia

Nov. 12, 1993
A-213, Kewal Park
Azadpur, Delhi-33

PREFACE TO SECOND EDITION

Homeopathy was born as a science, Dr. Hahnemann dreamt of making it a **"mathematical science in certainty." Dr. Kent** nourished the science with sincerity. He attached and developed principles which were meant to take the cause of Dr. Hahnemann towards his dream.

It seems from his writings that sometimes he fought alone with the adverse circumstances. The theory of 'Psora' was **jeered at** in his time.

But he continued his efforts of give a practical shape to this science of healing - and met a great success. His philosophy, his lectures on materia medica stand witness to all he did in his life.

The conditions in which he struggled to enrich this science can be imagined by the following words:

"At the present day there is only a very small number of homeopathic physicians that can come together in a body and say things that are worth listening to, a shamefully smaller number when we consider the length of time Hahnemann's books have been before the world."

- Dr. J.T. Kent

After Kent, Homeopathy expanded in volume, but the principles for which he lived his life were neglected to a great extent. **This supplement** is an effort to highlight the **various aspects** which were given importance by our **'Pioneer'**, and the readers will themselves see and analyses, how much we have advanced and in which direction.

Dr. K.D. Kanodia

May 16, 2006
A-213, Kewal Park
Azadpur, Delhi-33

PUBLISHER'S NOTE

Kent as a '**pioneer**' of Homeopathy cannot be missed by anyone in homeopathic profession. But his life and works are like an **Epic** which is to be studied again and again - and with different angles.

The more we study him, the more we get from him. The present work **brings us closer** to the great personality and if the readers feel satisfied with the material and presentation, our efforts shall be rewarded.

Kuldeep Jain

30.5. 2006 MD, B. Jain Publishers

ABOUT THE AUTHOR
Dr. K.D. Kanodia

Birth: Sept. 8, 1930

Education: Patna and Punjab Universities

Academic profile: BA (Hons.) MDSH, ND, DI Hom (The British Institute of Hom., London) MRSH (London).

Positions held & achievements:

- Author of about two dozen books on homeopathy, social and religious aspects.
- Edited monthly organ of Delhi Hom. Med. Association, New Delhi.
- Life member - DHMA New Delhi, IIPA New Delhi, Indian Red Cross Delhi, Accident Relief Society (Regd.) Delhi, etc.
- Member - Internatonal Hom. League, Geneva, Asian Hom. Medical League, Trivandrum.
- Recipient, Appreciation Award in Homeopath from Board of Hom. System of Med., Delhi.
- Considerable Research Work done in Homeopathy and Ayurveda.
- Serving Homeopathy through Charitable Dispensaries and Renowned Hospitals.
- Appreciations from people of the country and abroad and also the State Chief Ministers, Governers, Vice Chancellors and Schloars of repute.

CONTENTS

1. Kent in the clinic 1
2. Kent and materia medica 13
3. Kent – how he saw at things 27
4. Kent – study of mental aspects 37
5. Kent and miasms 47
6. Kent and relationship of remedies 50
7. Kent – bold, frank and sincere 54
8. Kent about remedies – that fortify the patient's constitution while curing it 62
9. Kent and Nash – as pioneers 65
10. Kent and problem cases 71
11. Kent and grouping of medicines 79
12. Kent and deeper modalities 90
13. Kent – the shadow side 94
14. Homeopathy needs one more Kent 99
15. Personification – in homeopathy 103
16. Complementaries and inimicals at a glance 105
17. Arsenicum album 112
18. We expect 114
19. When I am gone! 116
20. Case and action 118
21. Fear, faith and love 120
22. Symptoms and spheres 122

1

KENT IN THE CLINIC

ABORTION

Fear will often cause abortion, but when *Aconite* is given early enough, it will check the abortion, that comes from fear.

ALBUMEN

Urine scanty and foetid, containing albumen, and blood corpuscles (*Apis*).

ASTHMA ATTACKS EVERYDAY

Asthmatic attacks at least once a day all her life, brought on by every bodily exertion, coition, especially by every satisfying meal. (*Asaf.*).

BLADDER IRRITATION

No remedy has a greater irritation in the bladder and along the urinary tract than *Belladonna*. The urging to urinate is constant.

BLEEDING ANUS – IN INFANTS

Allium cepa cures a ragged, sensitive condition of the anus, with bleeding, in infants.

BREAST PAIN

When the child is nursing, there is a pain in the opposite breast (*Borax*)

BRONCHITIS OF INFANCY

Ipecac. is especially the infant's friend and is commonly indicated in the bronchitis of infancy.

BURNING IN VAGINA

The woman has so much burning in the vagina that she persuades the physician to make a more careful examination than he has done. She says, it burns like coals of fire. (*Carb-an.*)

CARDIAC ASTHMA

This is a great remedy in asthma, especially cardiac asthma. (*Naja*).

CHILD WAKES UP FRIGHTENED

Aesculus is especially useful in children that rouse up in sleep frightened and in confusion, like *Lycopodium*.

CHILDREN'S DIARRHOEA

If you had a child with copious gushing, violently foetid stool, ameliorated by lying on the abdomen, and it will have another stool if lying any other way. *Podophyllum* would be the remedy.

COLIC OF INFANTS

Colic of infants when they are relieved by lying on the stomach, as soon as the position is changed, they begin to scream again. (*Coloc.*)

COLIC

Colocynth is without much fever, without much thirst, a pain in one spot. An intense colic in abdomen ameliorated by doubling up, ameliorated by bending across something hard, is *Colocynth*.

CORNS ON SOLES

Soles of the feet-sore to walk upon-due to centres of little corns. (*Ant-c.*)

COUGH AFTER EATING

It has cough especially after eating and drinking cold things. (*Dros.*)

COUGH AT PUBERTY

Green sickness that comes on with girls at the time of puberty and the years that follow it. There will be almost no menstrual flow, but a cough will develop, with great pallor. (*Ferr-met.*)

COUGH BETTER LYING ON ABDOMEN

There is a cough in *Baryta carb.* where he coughs and coughs and gets no relief until he lies on the abdomen; so long he lies on the abdomen, he is free from cough.

COUGH FROM ANXIETY AND LYING DOWN

Cough from thinking and from anxiety. (*Ambr.*)

Cough relieved by lying down. (*Mang.*).

COUGHING BETTER IN COLD PLACE

If he can lie in a cool room without much covering, he will go longer without coughing. (*Coc-c.*)

CRACKING OF FINGERS IN WINTER

Cracking and bleeding of the fingers in winter and from washing in cold water. (*Cist.*).

DELAY IN GRANULATION

Staph. is the remedy that will make granulation come immediately.

DIABETES

It has cured sugar in the urine and polyuria. (*Nat-s.*)

DIABETES

This remedy has had a reputation for curing diabetes and this is not to be wondered at when it is known to have cured the weakness, anemia, and copious watery urine and great thirst, also copious dense urine. (*Lac-v-d.*)

DIFFICULT BREATHING

Ant-t. with its difficult breathing is sick at the stomach.

DRYNESS IN THE VAGINA

Lyc. produces and cures dryness in the vagina in which coition becomes very painful.

EDEMA

The face is greatly swollen at times, the eyelids look like water bags, the vulva hangs down like a water bag, the abdominal walls are of great thickness, and pit upon pressure, and the mucous membranes in any part look as if they would discharge water if they were punctured. (*Apis*).

ERUPTIONS ON AND AROUND GENITALS

The eruptions of *Crot-t.* very often select as a location, the genital organs.

ERUPTIONS ON PALMS

Anagalis does upon the palms of the hands just what *Crot-t.* does upon the genitals.

GALL STONE COLIC

This remedy has cured gallstone colic. Practitioners, who know how to direct a remedy, relieve gallstone colic in a **few minutes.** We have remedies that act on the circular fibres of these little tubes, causing them to relax, and allow the stone to pass painlessly. When this pain is a shooting, stabbing, tearing, lancinating pain, extending through the back. *Chelidonium* will cure it.

GALL STONE COLIC

You put a dose of *Bell.* on his tongue, the spasm lets up, stone passes on, and there is no more trouble; in **fifteen minutes,** the gallstone colic is gone. (*Bell.*).

GASTRIC ULCER

Cadm-s. is a great remedy in the gastric irritation of Carcinoma, a great palliative, coffee ground vomiting.

GLANDS HARD

Glands become hard but seldom suppurate. (*Brom.*)

HEADACHE ON RETENTION OF URINE

In **fluoric acid,** if one does not attend to the desire to urinate, a headache comes on.

HEADACHE

Catarrh, the headache, and gastric symptoms all belong together. (*Ant-c.*)

HIVES

A single dose of a very high potency of *Kali-i.* will turn things into order in persons subject to these hives and they **will not come again.**

HORRIBLY OFFENSIVE ODOR

This horribly offensive odor that is so permeating is often cured by *Kali-p*. It has really one of the most penetrating odors, so much so that when a woman suffers from Leucorrhoea, the odor can be detected when she enters the room.

HURRIES TO STOOL AFTER MEAL

Every mouthful of food hurries him to stool; drinking water will often hurry him to stool. (*Aloes.*)

HYSTERICAL FAINTINGS AFTER COITION

Agaricus is useful for the symptoms which come on after coition in young, nervous married women, hysterical fainting after coition.

INFLAMED MAMMARY GLANDS

When the mammary glands are inflamed without any general symptoms, but merely an inflammation of the glands, give *Phytolacca*.

MENSTRUAL PAIN

Each woman is a law unto herself. In this remedy (*Cimic.*) the sufferings are during the menstrual flow as a rule.

MENTALLY UNDEVELOPED

A mental state is especially found under *Bar-c.*, in adults who have never developed beyond childhood, who have always remained children. A person reasons like a child, talks like a child, whimpers like a child, cries like a child, wants to be petted like a child; so it is in *Bar-c.*

MILK VOMITS IN CHILDREN

The child wakes up again, fills the stomach with milk which comes up again in a few minutes, partly in curd and partly liquid, and again there is awful exhaustion, deathly appearance and prolonged sleep (*Aeth.*).

OCCIPITAL HEADACHE

Sil. is the routine remedy for offensive foot sweat and periodic occipital headaches.

PAIN – SACRUM AND HIPS

This pain through the sacrum and into the hips, when walking, is a striking feature of *Aesc.*

POLYURIA DURING NIGHT

A marked feature of Lyc., and one of the most

prominent of all remedies, in **polyuria during the night.**

RASH ON FACE BEFORE MENSES

Rash comes out upon the face before menses (*Dulc.*).

RETENTION OF URINE AFTER LABOUR

Routine remedy for retention of urine after labour is *Causticum*.

RETENTION OF URINE IN INFANT

The retention of urine in infant is so commonly an *Aconite* condition that you will hardly ever need to use any other medicine.

SKIN HOT EVEN WITHOUT FEVER

Heat of the skin and dryness is without fever (*Aloes*).

SUDDEN BLINDNESS

During the process of labour, the patient suddenly becomes blind. (*Cupr.*)

SUPPRESSED MENSES

If she becomes over heated from exertion, such as from ironing or washing, a few days before the menstrual period, it will be suppressed. (*Bry.*).

TAKES COLD BEFORE MENSES

She seems to take cold when ever menstruation is coming on. (*Mag-c.*)

TONSILLITIS

Large indurated tonsils will be cured after *Bar-c.* has failed. (*Calc-fl.*)

TOOTHACHE

Oh, what a comforting remedy (*Acon.*) it is for toothache! It has been so useful in toothache that nearly every old lady nowadays knows enough to put a drop of *Acon.* on a bit of cotton and put it in the hollow tooth. It will quite often palliate.

TORN FROM GRIEF

Her grief has simply torn her to pieces. *Ign.* will quiet her and tide her over the present moment.

TUMOR ON THE CRANIUM

Calc-fl. has cured a fluctuating tumor on the cranium of the infants known as **cepa laematoma.**

VAGINA – FLATUS

Loud emission of flatus from vagina. (*Brom.*)

VOMIT AND PURGE AT THE SAME TIME

I have seen *Arg-nit.* patients vomiting and purging in the same moment, not vomiting one second and purging the next, but gushing out both ways and with great exhaustion like cholera morbus, so relaxed, prostrated and weak.

Remarks: Besides his talented literary works and compilations, Dr. Kent's genius as a prescriber ranks him on the top of our pioneers.

His clinical observations are not limited to individuals, to a particular time or to a particular place or region. The above few examples will show that his experiences will meet the need of common man, mediocre physician, and also the talented persons in the field to deal with simple and even the most difficult cases.

2

KENT AND MATERIA MEDICA

ACONITE

- Aconite is more frequently indicated in *women and children* than in men.

- Sometimes it is true, it will *appear* to you that *Aconite* is capable of coping with all there is in the disease. *But* there seems to be a **lingering** something that holds on, and such medicines as *Arn.* and *Bell.* and *Ip.* and *Bry.*, do have to come in to *finish up the attack* – or sometimes *Sulphur.*

NATRIUM MURIATICUM

Delights to dwell upon the past unpleasant occurrences and lies awake at night thinking about them.

ANACARDIUM

Many complaints ameliorated by eating.

ANTIMONIUM TART.

Antim tart. with its difficult breathing is sick at the stomach.

ARGENTUM MET.

All symptoms worse after sleep. Memory and reasoning faculties disturbed. **Pains drive him to walk.**

ASAFOETIDA

Asthmatic attacks at least once a day all her life, brought on by every bodily exertion, coition, especially by every satisfying meal.

BARYTA CARB.

There is a cough is *Bar-c.* where he coughs and coughs, and gets no relief until he lies on the abdomen, so long he lies on the abdomen, he is free from cough.

BELLADONNA

- All his pains are **worse** from motion, worse from light, worse from a jar, worse from cold, He wants to be wrapped up warmly, and is worse from any exposure or a draft.

- Whenever we have checked secretions, we have fever, and in Bell., this is marked. Maddening headache with **suppressed catarrh.**

BERBERIS VUL.

Of course in all of the gouty states, we must look to the liver and kidneys for pains and various distresses; they are centres of observation, because these organs are more or less disturbed. And very often cardiac troubles go along with them. The kidneys, liver and heart are more or less disturbed in their functions and we see that Berberis takes hold of these organs.

BRYONIA

- Bryonia is often indicated in **injuries** of joints where Arnica would be a failure.

- It is **common** for Bryonia to be ameliorated from cold air, from cool applications. But, there are **rheumatic** complaints of Bryonia which are better from heat.

- In the Bryonia headaches, as well as rheumatic attacks, if he can perspire freedly, he will get relief. Bryonia is ameliorated in all its complaints as soon as the perspiration becomes free and general.

CACTUS

There is never an equal circulation of blood in the body; it is spasmodic and irregular, disturbed by contractions of circular fibres everywhere. When this comes in places where it can be felt, and realized by the senses, it is felt as contractions, as if caged in wires, and this gives us the key to *Cact*.

CALADIUM

Calad. has a number of times turned the patient entirely away from his cigar, and removes the overwhelming craving that prevents smokers breaking off their habit.

CALCAREA CARB.

- Children who cannot take lime from their natural food – born with an inability to digest the lime that is in their natural food, and they grow fat and flabby, and produce deficient bones. A solitary dose of sufficiently potentized remedy. Health comes, beauty, a growth of hair, better skin, better nails.

- Sweat of the head on slightest exertion; also his head is covered with cold sweat, when he is comfortable. The same things is true about the feet. When his feet become cold, they will sweat. When they are warm, they will sweat.

- Suppose the **patient always** avoided warm things, and much clothing, and wanted the cold open air, and still had a dozen keynotes, you will find every time that *Calc.* would fail.

CALCAREA PHOS.

Convulsions of children; but the remedy must be given when not in the convulsions, to secure the best effect.

CAPSICUM

Thirst after every dysenteric stool, a sudden craving for ice cold water, which causes chilliness.

CAMPHOR

When he is cold, he must uncover, even in a cold room. A flash of heat comes on and then he wants the covers on.

STAPHYSAGRIA

The *Staphysagria* patient when excited will keep up a constant swallowing and this goes on until it becomes a source of great annoyance.

CHAMOMILLA

Face **sweats after eating** or drinking. It is common feature of this remedy to sweat only about the head, the hairy scalp.

CHINA

You will cure more cases of intermittent fever with Ipecac. and *Nux-v.* than with *China*. *China* has **well defined chill,** fever, and sweat.

COCCULUS INDICA

The whole economy is slowed down, inactive.

COCCUS CACTI

If he can lie in a cool room without much covering, he will go longer without coughing.

COLOCYNTH

Some remedies select the muscles and tendons, some bones and periosteum, while others select the great trunks in which to manifest their symptoms. The pains of *Coloc.* appear, as a rule, in the larger nerves.

CONIUM

- The sufferings and conditions are better by letting the limbs hang down.
- He sweats copiously during **sleep.**

DIGITALIS

Now remember the liver and the heart symptoms, the jaundice, the slow pulse, the awful sinking in the stomach, the enlargement of the prostate gland, the gray stool, and you have the principal symptoms of *Dig.*

DULCAMARA

- Chronic recurrent dysentery from cold. If they have a dose of *Dulc.*, it **fortifies** them against the continual taking of cold.

EUPATOREUM PERF.

The most prominent symptoms are the vomiting of bile, aching of the bone as if they would break, the pains in the stomach after eating, and the nausea from the thought and smell of food.

FLUORIC ACID

- It corresponds to over heated states of the system, old cases of nightly fevers, coming on week after week, and year after year.

- There is a state in which a man is never satisfied with one women, but continually changes and goes from bad to worse until he is debauchee.

GELSEMIUM

Gels. is remedy for warm climates, while *Acon.* is a remedy for colder climates.

GLONOINE

Such medicines as *Op.* and *Glon.* relieve the blood pressure when symptoms agree. They equalize the circulation and the patient may not die.

HEPAR SULPH.

- Sweating all night without relief belongs to a great many complaints of *Hep*.

- Chilly, oversensitive to impressions, to surroundings, and to pain. Eruptions are sensitive to touch. The *Hep.* patients faint with pain, even from slightest pain. Tendency to suppurate and heals slowly.

HYDRASTIS

The headaches are only such as generally belong to stomach disorders, and prolonged nasal catarrh.

HYOSCYAMUS

Hyos. has such sensitive nerves all over the body in the skin that he cannot bear the clothings to touch the skin, and he takes it off.

HYPERICUM

It prevents Tetanus.

IGNATIA

Thirst when you would not expect it. **Thirst** during chill but non during the fever.

IODINE

- Iodine has the impulse to kill, not from anger, not from any sense of justice, but without any cause.
- Inspite of the hunger and much eating, he still emaciates.

KALIUM CARB.

The catarrhal state has settled in the chest and there is a chronic tendency to take cold.

KALMIA

It has palpitation, shaking the whole frame, audible, vehement palpitation. He cannot lie in his left side. Very slow pulse.

KREOSOTE

- Excoriating discharges, pulsating all over the body, profuse bleeding from small wounds, the three special characteristics of *Kreos.*

- A marked feature of the *Kreos.* constitution is that when the desire to urinate comes he must hurry or urine will escape.

LACHESIS

- Pulsating headache is part of a general pulsation from head to foot. In all arteries and inflamed parts there is pulsation. It is seldom that you will see *Lach.* headache without cardiac difficulty.

- It is a general feature of *Lach.* to be relieved from discharges.

LEDUM

Ledum is to whisky what *Calad.* is to smoking habit.

LILIUM TIG.

Extremely nervous, has fluttering of the heart, pain down the spine, and more or less prolapsus, with great sense of dragging down.

MANGANUM

- There is a history of a long period of scanty menstruation, or the menses have been delayed, until the patient was eighteen or twenty years of age.

- All the pains and aches in the upper part of the body **settle in the ears.** The pain in the throat shoots to the ears. There are pains in the throat and pain in the teeth that go to the ears. Pains in the eyes that centre in the ears.

- Cough is ameliorated by lying down.

NAJA

- *Naja* has more nervous, *Lach.* more septic symptoms.

- This is a great remedy in asthma, especially cardiac asthma.

NATRIUM SULPH.

- It causes the liver to make healthy bile which is the **natural solvent of gallstones,** when given in homeopathic doses at long intervals. It has cured many cases of gall stone colic. It has removed gall stones in many cases.

- It has cured sugar in the urine and polyuria.

NUX MOSCH.

Dazed – complete loss of memory, always ready to go to sleep; dry mouth, thirstless, chilly, constipated.

PODOPHYLLUM

It is a common feature after giving a high potency of *Podo.* in a diarrhea, that a **headache** comes on after diarrhoea is stopped. **It means** that the medicine has acted suddenly and the headache will pass away soon.

PULSATILLA

She cannot lie on the back without having a desire to urinate.

SEPIA

- Absence of intellectual lines and angles.

- When these symptoms group themselves together–the gnawing hunger, the constipation, the dragging down, the mental condition, it is *Sep.* and *Sep.* only. One is not sufficient, but it is the combination.

STAPHYSAGRIA

If often happens that nervous women soon after marriage are attacked with frequent and painful urging to urinate which becomes extremely troublesome and may last many days. *Staph.* is very comforting to the young wife.

TUBERCULINUM

A person gradually running down, never finding the right remedy, or relief only momentarily; has a constant desire to change, and travel, and go some where, and do something different, or to find a new doctor. Such condition belongs to one who needs Tuberculinum.

Remarks: Each materia medica has its speciality. It speaks of something new, highlights something uncommon and precious. Kent's 'Lectures' have their own attraction. They are not *mere compilations*. They tend to *personify the drugs.* They present the physical, mental and emotional aspects of men and medicines. Besides, his lectures are full of such knowledge about various related aspects that a student and a scholar both find it as a 'treasure' to understand, to remember and to follow and to be inspired during their journey of achievements.

UN – STABLE MIND

A person gradually running down, never finding the right remedy, or relief only momentarily; has a constant desire to change, and travel and go somewhere, and do something different, or to find a new doctor. The desire to travel, that cosmopolitan condition of mind belongs so strongly to one who needs Tuberculinum.

Dr. J.T. Kent.

3

KENT – HOW HE SAW AT THINGS

CHOICE OF PROPER REMEDY

Knowing all that I know if such a trouble should come upon to me, and I could not find the remedy to cure it, I would bear with it patiently, knowing I was keeping a much less grievance. Nor could I advice my patient to have a thing done that I would not have done upon myself.

CLINICAL OBSERVATIONS

You do not get all these things in the text, you have to see them applied. But the things I gave you that are brought out clinically, are those things, that have come from applying the symptoms of the remedy at the bed side to sick folks.

DANGER ABOUT CONSTITUTIONAL MEDICINE

Do not give that constitutional medicine that should have been administered to these patients twenty years ago, because there is not reaction enough in the life of the patient to turn him into order, **and he will be destroyed.**

EXPERIENCED PHYSICIANS

Experienced physicians learn to **classify patients by appearance.**

EXPLORATIONS INCOMPLETE

There may be conditions in the human race that we as yet, know no medicine for. We see certain groups of peculiar symptoms frequently repeat themselves, and we know they are representative of state of the economy, but up to this day, **we may not have seen** in the materia medica, their **counterpart. In medicines we have the exact counterpart for the diseases of the human race.**

HIGH POTENCIES CAN KILL

High potencies are means of tremendous harm, as well as tremendous good. It is better to know what you have done, **if you have killed your patient,** than to be ignorant of it **and go on and kill some more in the same way.**

HOMEOPATHIC FAILURES ARE WORST

The homeopathic failures are the worst failures on earth. Remedies only partly related to the case will change the character of the sickness so that no one can cure the case.

HUNTING AROUND FOR REMEDIES

In this way, a very **poor prescriber** may hunt around and get one remedy for one group of symptoms and another remedy for another group, and the patient is worse off than before. If the remedies are similar as to their **general nature,** then the little superficial symptoms are not so extremely important.

INDIVIDUALIZATION

Homeopathy is a matter of individualization as to how complaints spread. Some complaints begin on the right side and spread to the left. Some complaints begin in the top of the body and go downwards.

IT REQUIRES YEARS TO CURE

But the cure requires years and the patient must

be treated in the interim and according to his symptoms. The hay fevers will only be cured if the patient is curable, but if not, if his constitution is so **broken down, that he is incurable,** his hay fever will not be cured.

KNOWLEDGE ONLY PARTIAL TILL NOW

We have only a knowledge of **a few remedies** in each kingdom.

MAN AND MEDICINE

Every medicine has a **sphere of action, a peculiar nature where it differs from all other medicines,** and hence it becomes suitable to complaints of one class and not suitable to those of another. It is like nature of **human beings as they differ from each other,** and also like the nature of diseases, which differ from each other in character.

MEDICINES HAVE MANY ASPECTS

Every medicine must be observed as to its velocity, as to its pace, as to its periodicity, as to its motion, and its wave.

MOST IMPORTANT PART OF PROVING

That which he wishes belongs to that which he wills, and the things that relate to what he wills are the most important things in every proving.

PAROXYSMS – VERY IMPORTANT

The time for the administration of the dose is at the **close of paroxysm.** You get the best effect when reaction is at the best, and that is, when reaction is setting in, after a paroxysm has passed off. That is true of every paroxysmal disease where it is possible to wait until the end.

PRECAUTIONS IN HOMEOPATHY

Homeopathy will rule out such things as are **inimical** to the remedies and **inimical** to the patients in general, or do not agree with a particular constitution. I only speak of these things to impress upon you the **importance of feeding and treating your** patient in accordance with the remedy; in accordance **with a principle, and not by rule,** do not have a list of foods for your patients; **do not have a list of things for every body. There is no such thing in homeopathy.**

PROVER'S RISK DURING PROVINGS

The taking of more of the drug to prove it, does not do so much harm, provided the one who is directing the proving realizes when the symptoms begin to rise, and then stops the drug. Now if we go on with the proving by repeating the doses, after symptoms come on, we force the drug into the economy when he is already poisoned, and by this means we get a confusion in the symptoms, the **drug disease engrafted upon that individual for life.**

PROVING OF A MEDICINE

A medicine may be said to be thoroughly proved when it has left its impress upon all elements of man. When it has affected his memory and his intellect, when it has affected his organs and all their functions, i.e., when healthy man has taken a medicine until all these things are affected and the results are known as to the effects of that medicine. Every medicine affects in some way, all these elements of man, and no medicine is well proved until it is known that all these elements are affected.

PROVINGS – DIFFICULT – IMPERFECT

As provers do not follow up remedies until they produce these things, we have to gather them from the poisonous effects and clinical observations.

REAL ACTION OF A REMEDY

The medicine that covers the symptoms is the one *that will change the economy* from an abnormal to a normal state, the digestion will become orderly, and we will have growth and prosperity in the economy.

REMEDIES TALK AND TELL THEIR STORIES

By allowing remedies to talk and tell their own story, individualization is accomplished.

SNAP SHOT PRESCRIBING

A busy physician, who really and truly studies his materia medica, and has learnt the principles, will in time do a great deal of what seems to be snap shot prescribing, but he really does not do so, because he puts together many things **that outsiders would not think of.**

SPHERES OF REMEDIES

Some remedies select the muscles and tendons, some the bones and periosteum, while others select the great nerve trunks in which to manifest their symptoms.

STUDY OF FACES IN MEN AND MEDICINES

The study of faces of remedies is very profitable. We see these things in remedies as we see them in people.

STUDY OF HUMAN MIND

We do not know half as much about the human mind as we think we do.

SYMPTOMS – VERY IMPORTANT

One thing in homeopathy taught in Hahnemann's Organon is that unless there are symptoms to indicate the remedy, no great things should be expected from the administration of the remedy.

SYMPTOMS OF PROVINGS NOT ALWAYS ESSENTIAL

Though *Gels.* may not have produced Erysipelas, it will stop the progress of the disease in few hours, and the patient will go on to quick recovery. If we master thoroughly the materia medica, we do not stop to see if a remedy produces certain kind of inflammation, etc., but **we consider the state of the patient.**

SYMPTOMS

When the symptoms have been well gathered, the case is as good as cured, it is easy then to find a remedy. No remedy should ever be given on **one symptom.**

TALENTED PHYSICIAN – VERY SMALL IN NUMBER

At the present day there is only a very small number of homeopathic physicians that can come together in a body and say things that are worth listening to, a **shamefully smaller number** when we consider the length of time, Hahnemann's books have been before the world.

THE NOBLE PHYSICIAN

The noble, upright, truthful physician works in the night; he works in the dark; he works quietly, he is **not seeking for praise.**

WAY TO PRESCRIBE

In prescribing, I am in doubt whether there can be any such thing as a speciality, because the homeopathic physician prescribes for the patient. He prescribes for the patient, whether he has eye disease, or ear disease, or throat disease, or lung disease, or liver disease, etc.

WHIMS IN MEN AND MEDICINES

Medicines also have such queer whims. We must **study remedies as we would human character.**

Remarks: These are few extracts which are self explanatory and lead us to study and understand our great Pioneer. His 'lectures' are deep as an ocean. The more we read, the more we get. But this will facilitate the common reader to visualize things at a glance and enable him to go deeper for further studies.

4

KENT – STUDY OF MENTAL ASPECTS

ADULTS – WHERE MIND REMAINS UNDEVELOPED

This mental state is especially found under *Bar-c.*, in adults who have never developed beyond childhood, who have always remained children. A person reasons like a child, talks like a child, whimpers like a child, cries like a child, wants to be petted like a child, so it is in Bar-c.

ALWAYS RUNS TO NEW DOCTOR

A person gradually running down, never finding the right remedy or relief only momentarily, has a constant desire to change, and travel; and go somewhere, and do something different, or to find a new doctor. The desire to travel, that cosmopolitan condition of mind, belongs so strongly to the one who needs *Tub*.

ARGENTUM MET. AND INTELLIGENCE

It scarcely disturbs his affections; only makes slight and vague changes in his voluntary systems. But the memory, the intellectual part of man is disturbed increasingly to imbecility. In great sufferings – and it is full of sufferings – it affects his ability to reason. He is tired mentally and he forgets what he is talking about.

CEREBELLUM AND CEREBRUM

The cerebellum presides over respiration during sleep, and the cerebrum presides over respiration when the patient is awake. We might learn that from the provings of medicines if we never found it before.

CLASSIFICATION OF MENTAL SYMPTOMS

The mental symptoms can be classified in a remedy. The things that relate to the memory are not so important as the things that relate to the intelligence, and the things that relate to the intelligence are not so important as the things that relate to the affections or desires and aversions. That which he wishes belongs to that which he wills, and the things that relate to what he wills are the most important things in every proving.

DEBAUCHEE

If a young man cannot keep away from women, he is not so bad off if he will only keep to one, but he goes from one to many, until he stands on the street corners and in his lust, craves the innocent women that go along the street. (*Fl-ac.*).

EFFECTS OF FEAR ON WOMEN

It is very seldom that fear will give a man inflammation, but fear is a common cause of inflammation of the uterus, and of the ovaries, in plethoric, vigorous, excitable women.

EVILS OF MAN – ABSORBED BY PLANTS

The evils that are thrown by man may be absorbed by the vegetable kingdom. Plants will correspond to men in the region in which they grow, if there is anything in this.

EXPERIENCED PHYSICIANS

Experienced physicians learn to classify patients by appearance.

FACES OF REMEDIES

The study of the faces of remedies is very profitable. We see these things in remedies just as we see them in people.

HEART, LIVER, LUNGS AND MIND

You will be surprised to find that heart and liver affections are associated with hopelessness and despair. With every little trouble located in the heart there comes **hopelessness**, but when the manifestations of disease is in the lungs there is **hopefulness**.

IMPULSES AND DESIRES

In another patient, the thoughts jump into his mind and he cannot put them aside, and the thoughts are tormenting. An impulse is sometimes over whelming and over balances the mind, and he commits suicide. **Desires are of the will; impulses comes into the thoughts.**

IMPULSIVE INSANITY

These impulses are seen in cases of impulsive insanity; an insanity in which there is an impulse to do violence and strange things, and when the patient is asked why he does these things, he says he does not know. The patient may not be known to be insane in anything else; he may be a good *businessman. Remedies also have this.*

It is recorded under *Hep.* that a barber had an impulse to cut the throat of his patron with the razor while shaving him. The *Nux-v.* patient has an impulse to throw her child into the fire, or to kill her husband whom she dearly loves. The thought comes into her mind and increases until she becomes actually insane and beyond control and the impulse is carried into action. A *Nat-s.* patient will say "Doctor, you do not know how I have to resist killing myself. An impulse to do it comes into my mind." *Iod.* has the impulse to kill, not from anger, not from any sense of justice, but without any cause.

INSANITY OF WILL

- The highest love is the love of life; and when an individual ceases to love his own's life, and is weary of it, and loathes it, and wants to die, he is on the borderline of insanity. In fact, that is an **insanity of the will.** You have only to look with an observing eye to see that one may be **insane in the affections,** or insane in the intelligence. One may remain quite intact, and the other one be destroyed.

- Some persons lie awake at night and long for death, and there is no reason for it. That is a state of the will, insanity of the will.

INTELLECT AND WILL

Think what a state it is for a man who has been in good condition of health, respected in his business circles to have a desire to commit suicide.

You will see other kinds of insanity and a breaking down or a state of feebleness of the intellect, he cannot think nor reason; his affections are practically intact, but he finally goes into a state of imbecility, or he becomes wild and *commits suicide from impulse.*

That is an instance where the intellect has been affected first, and *spreads to the will.* Sometimes this state comes on, and no disturbance in the man's intellectual nature has been observed, it is intact, it is sound.

He has been sound in his business affairs, he has been a good father, he has been observed by those around him to be intelligent, but he has been silently brooding over his state and his hatred of the world, he has told nobody of it, and then he has been found hung in his room. **The man's intellectual nature keeps the man in contact with the world, but his affections are largely kept to himself.** A man can have affections for all sort of things and perversions of the affections, but his intellect will guide him not to show his likes and dislikes to the world. **The affections cannot be seen, but man's intellect is subject to inspection.** He cannot conceal his intellect.

MELANCHOLIA

If you examine those medicines that act primarily **on the liver,** that slow down the action of liver, you will find the word "melancholia." With heart troubles, great excitement. With liver troubles, slowing down of the mental state, inability of the mind to work.

MEN AND MEDICINES – BOTH HAVE DIFFERENT NATURE

Every medicine has a sphere of action, a peculiar nature whereby it differs from all other medicines and hence it becomes suitable to complaints of one class and not suitable to those of another. It is like the nature of human beings, as they differ from each other, and also like the nature of diseases, which differ from each other in character.

MENTAL STATES ALTERNATE WITH RHEUMATISM

- Mental states following the disappearance of rheumatism is a strong feature.
- Woman will come to you with one group of symptoms today and may come back to you with an entirely different group in a couple of weeks. (*Cimic.*)

MENTAL SYMPTOMS

Now, as the mental symptoms are the most important in a proving, so are the mental symptoms in sickness, the most important. Hahnemann directs us to pay most attention to the symptoms of the mind, because the symptoms of the mind constitute the man himself.

MIND DWELLS UPON

- Compelled to sit and dwell upon the most disagreeable things that force themselves upon him and he cannot get rid of them. (*Ambr.*)
- She delights to dwell upon past unpleasant occurrences and lies awake at night thinking about them. (*Nat-m.*)

PRETENDING SICKNESS

She would be in a hysterical condition for hours when anyone was looking at her. When she thought no one was near, she would getup, walk about, look in the mirror to see how handsome she was, but when she heard a foot on the steps, she would lie on the bed and appear to be unconscious. She would bear much pricking and you could scarcely tell she was breathing. (*Plb.*).

THE EXPERT PHYSICIAN

- The expert physician often sees all these symptoms in the **twinkling of an eye.** The action of the patient, a word dropped by the nurse and what he has observed himself will all have shown him the remedy.

VIOLENT DREAMS

- With all the cardiac remedies, we have violent dreams, great excitement of the brain during sleep, waking up started and frightened, very commonly with a feeling of falling. Dreams of falling.

WILL AND UNDERSTANDING

- Whenever a medicine makes a man desire to do something it affects his will, and when it affects his intelligence it is acting on his understanding. Medicines act on both.

Remarks: Kent as we have seen above, touches all aspects of mind – and also co-relates them with such phenomenon in the world of medicines. The deep analysis at many places are a source of vast knowledge for the reader as also it renders insight to those interested to explore further in the field.

BOUNDARIES

Saints and incarnations are beyond the boundaries of caste and creed, scientists are beyond the boundaries of space, scholars and poets are beyond the boundaries of time, and homeopathic potencies are beyond the boundary of chemical laws.

5

KENT AND MIASMS

Psora is the beginning of all physical sickness. All the diseases of man are built upon *Psora*. Psora is the *primitive* disorder of the human race. It is the disordered state of the internal economy of the human race.

Psora goes to the very primitive wrong of the **human race,** the very first sickness of the human race, that is, the **spiritual sickness.**

If we regard Psora as *synonymous with itch,* we **fail to understand** and fail to express there by, anything like the original *intention of Hahnemann*.

If any sickness ran longer than six weeks, it would be placed among the *sub-acute,* if it ran on indefinitely, it was called chronic. But a *chronic miasm is chronic from its beginning,* and an acute miasm is acute from its beginning.

The complicated forms of *Psora are those that are inherited.*

Hahnemann says, "Psora is the oldest miasmatic chronic disease known. The oldest history of the oldest nation does not reach its origin."

Some persons will say that acarus is prior to the eruption, but they do not know that a healthy person will not be affected by the acarus. It is the state that is prior, the itching is not prior.

Thinking, willing and acting are the three things that make up the sickness of the science of the life of the human race. Man thinks, he wills, and he acts. All diseases upon the earth, acute and chronic are representatives of *man's internals.*

Thinking and willing establishes a state in man that identifies the condition he is in. As long as man continued to think that *which was* true and held that which was good to neighbour, that which was *uprightness and justice,* so long man remained upon the earth free from susceptibility to disease because that was the state in which he *was created*.

Psora was not due to actions of the body, as *we find Syphilis and Sycosis* to be, but it is due to an influx from a state. As Psora piles up generation after generation, century after century, the susceptibility to it increases.

Kent, at least apparently differs in many ways from what has been told by *Hahnemann* in his chronic diseases. Hahnemann has told that Psora is most contagious. *The physician while feeling the pulse hurriedly* may be infected from the patient with Psora which thus enters into deep interior, and no wash from outside can undo that touch.

Dr. J.C. Burnett differs still more when he says that no amount of potentized remedies can kill the acarus, and they are required to be *killed on the spot*.

Whatever and wherever the differences may be, one thing is true that if the outer manifestations of skin are suppressed, they give rise to more serious ailments and the internal organs suffer great damage.

6

KENT AND RELATIONSHIP OF REMEDIES

Kent was the only 'Pioneer' in homeopathy who *understood and declared the delicacies* of relationships in medicines. He boldly told what he saw and whatever he saw-was very deep – all scientific, all analytical, all practical. He was forceful in what ever he told. He enjoyed in whatever he told. It was like *Wm. Wordsworth who saw daffodils and found a fountain of joy;* "And then my heart with pleasure fills. And dances with the daffodils." He was never sorry for what he saw and what he told.

This we can appreciate when we read Dr. E.B. Nash. He says regarding alternation of *Rhus-t.* and

Hyos. – which gave him very good result, and which he appreciated also, for their performing wonders for him. But lastly, he concludes, "This is the only *alternation I am ever guilty of.* It is like that of Hahnemann when he alternated Bryonia and Rhus tox in fevers." *But Hahnemann* never said that he ever felt *guilty of alternating!* It was like *R. Herrick* who saw the same '*Daffodils* that Wm. Wordsworth saw, but expressed it differently, "Fair daffodils, we weep to see, You haste away so soon." Dr. Nash never saw the wonders of alternation from a scientific angle, from an analytical approach or even a deeper insight. He could not recognize the delicacy of *relationships in remedies.*

Now let us see how *Kent* presents the *phenomenon of relationship.*

1. After practicing a while, you will be surprised to observe the *pendulum* – like action between heat and cold in various *complementary* remedies. *Fl-ac.* not only antidotes the abuse of *Sil.* but also follows the *Sil.*

2. *Sil.* is the natural follower of *Puls.,* and you would be astonished to know how often a patient leaving

Puls. runs towards *Sil. Sil.* goes deeper into the case, it does more curing, and it is the *natural chronic of Puls.*

3. Then it is that this medicine. (*Fl-ac.*) comes in the series. *Fl-ac.* follows *Sil.* as naturally as *Sil.* follows Puls.

4. *They exist in threes. There are other remedies that exist in threes,* but the most common ones you will think of will be *Sulph., Calc.* and *Lyc.; Sulph., Sars.* and *Sep.;* and *Coloc., Caust.,* and *Staph.,* which often *follow each other and rotate in this way.*

Remarks: Here Dr. Kent shows himself as a real follower and scientific analyzer of Dr. Hahnemann's teachings. Dr. Hahnemann in his *'Chronic Diseases'* has clearly indicated symptoms in a routine or mechanical way, but he *perceived* the sphere of the remedies in alternation in all the 183 cases although **they differed in symptoms** and many other apparent aspects from each other. Even Dr. M.L. Tyler and Dr. E.A. Farrington – as quoted by Dr. M.L. Tyler have **not been able to appreciate the delicacy.**

Relationship plays an important and vital role in all walks of life and this is equally so in medicines also. There are hundreds of such occasions when Dr. Kent has drawn our attention to such features and his contributions are a valuable treasure for the homeopaths.

BEAUTIFYING MAMMARY GLANDS

Saw Palmetto, besides its well written up action on the prostate gland, can now take its stand as a beautifying remedy, since it promotes in a marked degree, the growth of mammary glands in women.

Dr. Dewey.

7

KENT – BOLD, FRANK AND SINCERE

Dr. Kent says in his 'Lectures', "We owe no obedience to man *not even to our parents,* after we are old enough to think for ourselves. We *owe obedience to truth."*

And this 'Truth' sparkles everywhere is his writings. He speaks of his *own weaknesses* with the same ease, with which he speaks the *limitations* of the science of homeopathy which he practiced.

AN OLD CASE
In an old case, a cure can never be promised.

BEWARE OF PHOSPHORUS IN IMPOTENCY

Beware of giving it in impotency or in weakness, as this is often associated with very feeble constitutions and Phos. not only fails to cure, but seems to add to the weakness. Phos. will set patient to running down more rapidly who are suffering from a vital weakness, who are always tired, simply weak, always prostrated, and want to go to bed.

CANCER CURE

Any one who goes around boasting of the cancer cases he has cured ought to be regarded with a suspicion.

CONSCIENTIOUS AND HUMANITARIAN

Knowing all that I know, if such a trouble should come upon me, and I could not find the remedy to cure it, I would bear with it patiently, knowing I was keeping a much less grievance. Nor could I advice my patient to have a thing done that I would not have done upon myself.

CONSUMPTION CURE

Do not believe or think favourably of cures for consumption. Hardly any one who knows any thing about it can conscientiously present a consumption cure to the world.

CURING INCURABLES

You need not believe things, you are not obliged to. But think about them, and some day after practicing a while, and making **numerous mistakes in attempting to cure incurables,** you will admit the awful power of homeopathic medicines.

DANGERS IN UNSCIENTIFIC PROVINGS

If we go on with the proving by repeating the doses, after symptoms come on, we force the drug into the economy when he is already poisoned, and by this means, we get **confusion in the symptoms,** the drugs disease **engrafted upon that individual for life.**

EXAMINING A CHILD

The *child is like the animal.* You never have to ask a horse or dog where he feels pain, because he will always tell by his motions. So does the infant.

EXPLORATIONS INCOMPLETE

There may be conditions in the human race that

we, as yet, know no medicine for. We see certain groups of peculiar symptoms frequently repeat themselves, and we know they are representatives of state of the economy, but upto this day, we may not have seen in the Materia Medica their counterpart. **In medicines we have the exact counterpart for the diseases of the human race.**

HIGH POTENCIES CAN KILL

High potencies are means of tremendous harm as well as of tremendous good. **It is better to know** what you have done, **if you have killed your patient,** than to be ignorant of it and go on and *kill some more in the same way.*

HOMEOPATHIC FAILURES

The homeopathic failures are the worst failure on earth. Remedies only partly related to the case will change the character of the sickness so that no one can cure the case.

IGNORANCE – ACCEPTED

We do not know half as much about the human mind as we think we do.

PROFITABLE BUSINESS

It is quite a profitable business for one who has not much conscience and not much intelligence. But a **conscientious physician** feels worried and knows he is not doing what he ought to do for his patient, unless he reaches out for the remedy which touches the constitution.

PROVINGS – IMPERFECT

As provers do not follows up remedies until they produce these things, we have to gather them from the poisonous effects and clinical observations.

PROVINGS WASTED

The great bulk of the *Thuja provings have been wasted,* because there is so much confusion in the great number of symptoms. While the earlier provings brought out many of the characteristics, the Vienna provings, to a great extent, confused the image of Thuja.

REMEDIES NOT WELL RECORDED

Many of our remedies are not well recorded; they have not yet *been observed in their alternations,* and marked as such.

SEEMING CURE-WHERE DANGEROUS

We read in the text that 'Ferrum' is a remedy for **diarrhea** in the last stage of consumption. Well, sometimes it is, *if the patient is prepared to die*. Ferr. will stop the diarrhea but after it is stopped, the *patient will not live long*.

SILICEA GREATLY INJURES

There are cases that would be greatly injured by so deep a remedy as *Sil.* if given in the beginning, that is, the suffering would be unnecessary; but if you commence with *Puls.* you can mitigate the case and *prepare it to receive Sil.,* provided the two would appear to be on a plane of agreement.

TALENTED PHYSICIANS — FEW IN NUMBER

At the present day, there is only a very small number of homeopathic physicians that can come together in a body and say things that are worth listening to, *a shamefully small number* – when we consider the length of time, Hahnemann's books have been before the world.

THE IDEAL PHYSICIAN

The noble, upright, truthful physician works in the night, he works in the dark, he works quietly, he is **not seeking for praise.**

TONSILLITIS

Two or three times I have absolutely **failed to cure** with remedies **selected to the best of my ability** and they have gone to the surgeon and he has cut them off, but I believe these tonsils ought to be all cured.

WELL PROVED MEDICINES

Every medicine affects in some way all these elements of man and **no medicine is well proved until** it is known how all these elements are affected.

IT WOULD TAKE A CENTURY TO CONFIRM

Lac-c. is in its beginning yet, although it has made some marvellous cures, but many of its symptoms are doubtful, and it would **take a century to confirm them.**

Comments: Dr. Kent studies medicine deeply and his observations are rare and important. He never hesitated to tell the truth. He spoke in the interest of the 'pathy' as well as in the interest of patients. Welfare of the people was his aim. He never told that I have cured this sickness. He always declared the marvels that a remedy can create. He analysed things in a wider context, in the longer interest of the science and philosophy. He is always to be read with this background in mind to get the best from him.

PERMANENT CURE THROUGH HOMEOPATHY

A cure can be rapid, gentle, sure and without any after – sufferings, but the word 'permanent' may be simply misleading. The causes that created the sickness can again cause the same sickness. How can any system claim to cure permanently in all cases. Even persons may remain healthy all their life without the aid of any remedy what so ever – if the vital force in their case is active enough to deal with environmental susceptibilities.

KENT ABOUT REMEDIES – THAT FORTIFY THE PATIENT'S CONSTITUTION WHILE CURING IT

CALCAREA CARBONICA

Children – who cannot take lime from their natural food- born with an inability to digest the lime that is in their natural food, and they grow fat and flabby and produce deficient bones. A solitary dose of sufficiently potentized remedy. **Health comes,** *beauty, a growth of hair, better skin, better nails.*

DULCAMARA

Chronic recurrent *dysentery* from cold. If they have a dose of Dulc., it **fortifies** them against the continual taking cold.

MANGANUM

It is also a great liver remedy. There is congestion and tumefaction of the liver. It has cured a tendency to fatty degeneration. It has cued many cases of gall stones; which means that the liver goes into such a sluggish state that the **bile is unhealthy,** the flow is impeded, and then little nodules form in it, and *form gall stones.* It establishes a *better working* order of the stomach – a *better working* basis of the liver, the **bile becomes healthy,** and gall stones are dissolved in the healthy bile.

NATRIUM MURIATICUM

Nat-m. not only removes the tendency to intermittents but restores the patient to health and takes away the tendency to colds, the susceptibility to colds, and to periodicity. **It is the susceptibility that is removed.**

Comments: Dr. Kent also approves remedies as *preventive* when he says, "A remedy will not have to be *so similar* to prevent disease as to cure it."

He is *too clear* about the cures when he says, "A few drugs will be similar enough to help, but only the *simillimum* will cure."

Simple compilations of informations are not enough. We read in the **nineteenth century** journals about the difficulties of *students crying for help.*

It is especiality of Dr. Kent. that he generalizes, visualizes and practices when he tries to individualise a case. This makes his contributions – *a treasure for all times to come.*

His deep studies and observations have explored things of lasting importance for the entire human race. He observes regarding *Nux-v.* and *Ign.* that, *"Europeans develop symptoms more often calling for Nux vom. in their hysterical manifestations, while Americans often need Ign."*

All this guide us for many more explorations in the field.

MIASMS IN HOMEOPATHY

The best study of miasms only lead us to 'simillimum'. Sulphur stands for *Psora*, Mercury for *Syphilis*, and Thuj. for *Sycosis*, and it is all *because* of *similimum*. There may be chain of remedies for each group and only 'similimum' can and does decide our selection.

9

KENT AND NASH – AS PIONEERS

Both were contemporaries, but were *poles apart* in their views. They did not even refer *each other* in their writings.

1. *Dr. Nash says,* "I do not believe in the so called incompatibles as some do. I should give *Caust.* after *Phos., Sil.* after *Merc.*, or *Rhus-t.*, after *Apis* if I found them indicated." And we know that *indication* is a vague term in homeopathy. **There is nothing like absolute indications.** *Inimicals* have to be considered while giving a remedy.

Dr. J.T. Kent has a very balanced view in this regard. He not only considers **inimicals** in the **medicines,** but **also in the diet of** *each patient* – individually, in relation to the *particular remedy* being administered to him. He also cautions for constitutional remedies during *paroxysms*. He then warns us that a cold bath will antidote the action of *Rhus-t.* or Calc. if taken just after taking the dose. *Such practical* hints cannot be seen in *Nash's Leaders*.

Although, Dr. Nash has mentioned at some places that a particular remedy is complementary to the other, e.g. "China is its (Carbo. veg's great complementary." But he has not *revealed* the **secrets of medicines** existing in *pairs* and *threes*.

Dr. Kent says about *pairs,* "When this remedy (*Eup-per.*) has been apparently indicated in intermittents, and it has not proved of sufficient depth to root out the intermittent, there are two remedies; either of which is likely to follow it, and these are *Nat-m.* and *Sep.* These two remedies are very closely related to *Eup-per.* and take up the work where it leaves off, when the symptoms agree.

Then he says, "Fl-ac. follows *Sil.* as naturally as Sil. follows *Puls. They exist in threes,* but the most common ones you will think of will be *Sulph., Calc.* and *Lyc., Sulph., Sars.* and *Sep.,* and *Coloc., Caust.,* and *Staph.,* which often follow each other and rotate in this way."

Then he advises, "There are cases that would be greatly injured by so deep acting a remedy as Sil. if given in the beginning, that is, the suffering would be unnecessary; but if you *commence with Puls.* you can mitigate the case and *prepare* it to receive Silica., provided the two would appear to be on the plane of agreement.

About Nux-v. and Sulph. he says, "Nux is closely related to sulphur and often **antidotes the over action of Sulph.** It seldom goes to the bottom and antidotes the constitutional action of *Sulph*, but it will remove its exaggerated action, its superficial action."

Such deeper aspects are not reflected in Nash.

2. Then, we find that Dr. Nash always appears to be a *lonely prescriber* – lost in few *solitary cases* which he claims, he has cured. He has not given a *wider field* where a common prescriber can get the benefit of the experiences. *Such spots are* very few. I quote Dr. Nash. "I remember a case of asthma of years standing to which I was called at midnight, because they were afraid the patient would die before morning. Found that her attacks always came at 1 a.m. Gave Ars. 30th and she was completely cure by it."

The case *leaves* many ifs and buts when practically viewed in the *present context*. The glory of homeopathy shall touch the height when the prescriptions prove a guideline for lacs of patients and practitioners in the field. *In contrast,* we may read Dr. J.T. Kent, "You put a dose of *Bell.* on the tongue, the spasm lits up, stone passes on, and there is no more trouble; **in fifteen minutes,** the gall stone colic is gone."

Kent always stresses on the wonders of a dose – which it can perform. Nash finds an occasion to show that he has achieved a result.

In the one, we find some *exploration,* in the other - some *attainment.* **One remains limited to the time, the other rises beyond the limits of time.**

4. Then we see that *Dr. Nash* is some times a *bitter critic*. About *Schuessler*, he says, "I have no faith in the *Schueslerian* theory in regard to it." It is true. But he might speak a word with regard to his contributions. *All his remedies* are being used in homeopathy in potencies and with *marvelous results*. Even his triturations are also found useful at many places.

We find that *Dr. J.T. Kent* has been very balanced in his opinions every where. We quote when he says about *Nat-p.* "We are not dependent upon Schuessler alone for indications for this remedy, as we have many pathogenetic symptoms. *Schuessler's indications were good and mostly confirmed by clinical observations.*"

5. We cannot, by any means *underrate* the importance of Dr. Nash, as his observations about *Antim crud.* and *Nux-v.* and few other remedies have been *superb at çertain places,* but we do not find the wide horizon in his thoughts to enlighten *generation after generation* – on a large scale as we find in the case of *Dr. J.T. Kent. Both were* devoted to their *professions, both lost their eye sight* at the old age, but Dr. J.T. Kent's contributions are vast in sphere – capable of inspiring and heading the profession, as well as the '*Pathy*' for *centuries and centuries.*

Remarks: The above comparison is only with *regard to some aspects.* It is not the purpose to *discuss in detail.* If we see them at a glance, we find *Dr. Nash as a talented prescriber,* and his sphere is *limited* to this part only. Dr. Kent on the other hand was a *genius* of high order and he covered a vast field in his achievements. His contributions on philosophy, materia medica and repertory are all memorable gifts of this dedicated soul. No single person has contributed to the science of homeopathy to this extent and with a literature of such high order.

WE CANNOT EXPECT

- We cannot expect uniform results on a mass scale with the Homeopathic doses, as we do not expect all the trees in the forest of similar height.

- We cannot expect all men to develop similar understandings as we do not expect all people to have exactly similar physical identities.

- We cannot expect to reform all people with sermons, as we do not expect every body to take similar food like animals of certain species.

- We cannot expect any so-called religion to be universal, as the religions are only labeling platforms – using stickers when the baby is born.

- We cannot expect peace in the world as the man is born in turmoil, grown in turmoil, and leaves the world in turmoil (Universal – Truth.).

10

KENT AND PROBLEM CASES

Kent has especiality in presenting his problem cases. He does not let them remain some 'solitary' individual cases. His cases are guidelines for all and for all times. Let us see:

BROMIUM CASES

They are found especially in those individuals that are made *sick from being heated.* It is also indicated in complaints that come on in the night after a very *hot day in the summer.* But *after complaint* comes on, no matter where it is, he is so sensitive to cold that a draft of cool air freezes him but he cannot be over heated without suffering.

BRYONIA IN INJURIES

Bryonia is often indicated in injuries of joints where Arnica would be a failure.

CACTUS – THE KEY TO USE

There is never an equal circulation of blood in the body; it is spasmodic and irregular, disturbed by contractions of circular fibres every where. *When this comes in places where it can be felt,* and realized by the senses, it is felt *as contractions,* as if caged in wires, and this gives us the *key to Cactus.*

CARDIAC WEAKNESS

There was a woman in this city who answered just such a description; her state was one of peculiar *cardiac weakness* with *dyspnoea and palpitation on motion.*

I continued to study the case, which was *extremely vague,* having nothing but those few symptoms, and finally I settled upon *Am-c.,* and she has been on this remedy for *eighteen months.* She now climbs mountains, she does everything she wants to do, and is about ready to go to house keeping. One dose generally acts upon her from *six weeks to two months,* steadily improving her each time.

CHANGE OF CLIMATE

Every year women bring their babies back from mountains, at the end of the season and then we get some Dulcamara cases.

DAY AND NIGHT AWAKE

Day and night she is wide awake, and with such sensitiveness to her surroundings that you would naturally think from what things she hears and how she is disturbed by noise, that she can hear the flies walk upon the walls and the clock striking upon he distant steeple.

You do not get all these things in the text, you have to see them applied. But the things *I give you that are brought out clinically* are those things that have come from applying the symptoms of the remedy **at the bed side to sick – folks.**

DEBAUCHEE

If a young man cannot keep away from women, he is not so bad off, if he will only keep to one, but he goes from one to many, until he stands upon the street corners and in his lust, craves the innocent women that go along the street. *Fl-ac.* is suitable in that state.

DIARRHOEA OF CHILDREN

If you had a child with copious, gushing, violently fetid stool, ameliorated by lying on the abdomen and it would have another stool if lying any other way, *Podo.* would be the remedy.

EPILEPSY

Congestions that come on suddenly. Convulsions *epileptiform* in character. You treat those with *Bell.;* the attack is relieved. After two or three attacks, Bell. will do no more and you are *worse off this time than you were before.* **Often it is a case that needs Calc.**

FLUCTUATING TUMOR ON THE CRANIUM

The chemical union of lime and Fluoric acid gives us a remedy with a *new nature and property.* However conversant one may be with either or both of these elements, he could not predict the curative powers held in this double remedy.

This remedy has cured a fluctuating tumor on the cranium of infants *known as Cephalaematoma.*

GOUTY STATES

Of course in all of the *gouty states* we must look to the liver and kidneys for pains and various distresses; they are centres of observation, because these organs are more or less disturbed in their functions and we see that *Berb. takes hold of these organs.*

HAY FEVER

I remember one time having occasion to prescribe Allium cepa at long distance. It was near a homeopathic pharmacy. I wired the pharmacist to send my patient *All-c.,* and he labeled it. Well, patient kept the bottle and used it next season, but it *did no good.*

That is likely to be the *case,* even when symptoms seems to agree., In a psoric condition, a short – acting remedy is insufficient; it may *help for one day only;* and the deep acting remedy that includes the patient as well as the hay fever and all other symptoms will have to be administered.

HIVES

A single dose of a very high potency of Kali-i. will turn things into order in persons subject to these hives and they will not come again.

HYDROCEPHALUS

He is not easily disturbed. He lies upon his back with limbs drawn up, often making automatic motions with the arms and legs. Sometimes, one side is paralysed, but the other keeps up *automatic motions.*

When *Hell.* was given, repair set in; *not instantly* but gradually. There comes a sweat, a diarrhea or vomiting – a reaction. *They must not be interfered* with, no remedy must be given. They are signs of reaction. If the child has vitality enough to recover, he will now recover. If the vomiting is stopped by any remedy, that will stop it, the *Hellebore* will be antidoted.

INSTANT RELIEF – GALL STONE COLIC

When this pain is a shooting, stabbing, tearing, lancinating pain, extending through to the back, *Chel.* will cure it. The instant it relieves, the patient says, "Why, what a relief; the pain has gone."

MELANCHOLIC GIRL

It is a strange thing to see a bright little girl of 8 or 9 years old taking on sadness, melancholy, and commencing to talk about the future world, and the angels, and that she wants to die and go there, and she is sad, and wants to read the bible all day. That is a strange thing; and yet *Calcarea has cured that.*

(**Note:** You can mark the way of Kent. He never says that I have cured the case. He always speaks – a particular medicine cured that case).

PARALYTIC STIFFNESS

It is entirely without inflammation. It is a sort of paralytic stiffness, a paralysis of the tired body and mind. A man will *stretch out his leg on a chair and he cannot flex it until he reaches* down with his hands to assist. (*Cocc.*).

PATHOLOGICAL CONDITIONS

Do not be discouraged in prescribing if the pathological conditions do not go away; but if all the symptoms of the patient have gone away, and the patient is eating well, and is sleeping well, and going well, do not feel that it is impossible for that opacity of the cornea to go away, for sometimes, it will.

PERVERTED LOVE

A *sensitive girl,* though she would not let any one but her mother know of it, falls in love with a married man. She lies awake nights, sobs. She says, "Mother, why do I do that, I cannot keep that man out of my mind."

Ign. enables her to control her emotions. **Nat-m. is its natural follower.**

SMOKING HABIT

Calad. has a number of times turned the patient entirely away from his cigar, and removes the overwhelming craving that prevents smokers *breaking off their habit.*

TEETHING CRISIS

Kreos. is a great remedy for diarrhea in the summer, especially for infants. Infants have troubles at the time of teething only because they are sick, and if the child were not in disorder, he would not have trouble when teething.

Remarks: The above are few examples of how Dr. Kent presents his experiences, so that they can be useful to most of the people at most of occasions.

KENT AND GROUPING OF MEDICINES

- 4 a.m. diarrhea: Aloe, Nat-s., Podo.
- All winter coryza: Carb-v., Cist., Graph.
- Amelioration from diarrhea: Abrot., Nat-s., Ph-ac.
- Anemia – menses suppressed: Ferr., Mang.
- Anus remedies: Alum., Caust., Graph., Nit-ac.
- Aphthae: Ars., Borx., Nit-ac., Sul-ac.
- Appendicitis: Arn., Bell., Bry., Rhus-t.
- Asthma from stomach disorders: Nux-v., Sang.
- Better cold bath: Arg-n., Led., Meph., Nat-m., Pic-ac., Puls.

- Better fast: Con., Nat-m.
- Better heat, better motion: Rhodo., Rhus-t., Ruta.
- Better lying on stomach: Acet-ac., Bar-c., Cina, Coloc., Med., Podo.
- Better move: Arg-met., Ferr., Fl-ac., Iod., Kali-i., Puls., Rhus-t.
- Better sleep: Phos., Pic-ac., Sep., Sil.
- Better warm drinks: Ars., Chel., Lyc., Sabad.
- Bleedings: Carb-v., Chin., Ip., Kreos., Millef., Phos., Sabin., Sec., Trill.
- Blows nose constantly: Hydr., Kali-bi., Psor., Sticta.
- Breasts dwindle: Con., Iod., Lyc., Nux-m., Sabal.
- Burning abscess: Anthraci., Ars., Pyrog., Tarent.
- Can breathe better when standing: Cann-s.
- Cannot breathe while standing: Psor.
- Cannot lie on left: Nat-m., Phos.
- Cannot lie on right: Mag-m., Merc.
- Cardiac remedies: Cact., Dig., Gels., Kalm., Latr., Lil-t., Nat-m., Sep., Spig.

- Cobweb sensation: Alum., Bar-c., Borx., Graph.
- Cold in patches: Calc.
- Colic better lying on stomach: Acet-ac., Cina., Coloc., Cupr., Med., Podo., Stann.
- Cough better by sip of water: Caust., Cupr.
- Craves eggs: Calc-c., Nat-p.
- Craves Lemon: Bell., Cycl., Nit-ac., Sabin.
- Crop of boils: Arn., Hep., Sil., Sulph.
- Croup trio: Acon., Hep., Spong.
- Diarrhoea – Beer: Aloe, Kali-bi.
- Diarrhoea – day: Petr., Podo.
- Discharges offensive: Ars., Bapt., Carb-v., Graph., Kali-p., Kreos., Phos., Podo., Psor., Pyrog.
- Disorderly state: Ars., Calc., Ip., Sep., Sulph.
- Do not disturb: Bry., Ph-ac.
- Dreams of falling from height: Cact., Dig., Thuj.
- Earache – children: All-c., Cham., Puls.

- Eczema face: Graph., Lyc.
- Eruptions – Bends: Graph., Nat-m., Sep.,
- Eruptions - patches: Petr.
- Eruptions suppressed: Bry., Cupr., Zinc.
- Eruptions: Anac., Clem., Corot., Ran-b., Rhus-t.
- Excessive sensitive: Cham., Coff., Nux-v.
- Excitable - disturbed: Bry., Cham., Coff., Ign., Nux-v.
- Ext. cold, int. burning: Calc., Camph., Carb-v., Led.
- Eye Strain: Graph., Nat-m., Paris, Ruta
- Feels hot without fever: Aloe, Fl-ac., Puls.
- Feels sore bruised: Arn., Bapt., Eup-per., Pyrog.
- Finger tips: Cist., Merc., Petr., Sep.
- Flabby fatty: Am-c., Ant-c., Asaf., Calc-c., Caps., Ferr-m., Graph.
- Flat breast: Iod., Lac-d., Lyc., Nux-m., Sabal.
- Flatus from vagina: Brom., Lyc., Sars.

- Frequent changes in symptoms: Cimic., Ign., Puls.
- Glands hard: Brom., Carb-an., Con.
- Greasy skin: Nat-m., Plb., Sel., Thuj.
- Hair falls – pubes: Nat-m., Nit-ac.
- Hard to hear human voice: Phos.
- Headache – hammering: Carb-v., Lach., Kali-bi., Kali-i., Sep.
- Heat in patches: Sulph.
- Hernia: Lyc., Nit-ac., Nux-v., Plb.
- High fever: Acon., Bell., Cham., Nux-v., Op., Phyt., Pyrog.
- Hoarseness: Alum., Carb-v., Caust., Lyc., Phos.
- Hot flatus: Agar., Aloe
- Hunger much: Abrot., Anac., Iod., Nat-m., Petr., Psor., Staph.
- Impulses: Ars., Hep., Iod., Nat-s., Nux-v.
- Injuries: Arn., Bell-p., Bry., Calen., Con., Hyper., Led., Nat-s., Rhus-t., Ruta, Staph., Stront., Symph.

- Itch without eruption: Alum., Ars., Dolic., Mez.
- Learning to walk (late): Bar-c., Nat-m.
- Leather-bag stomach: Ferr., Kali-bi., Sep.
- Leucorrhea offensive: Hep., Kali-p., Kreos.
- Leucorrhoea – little girls: Cann-s., Cub., Sep.
- Loud eructations: Arg-n., Asaf., Carb-v.
- Low mindedness: Fl-ac., Pic-ac., Sep.
- Low type fever: Ail., Bapt., Lach., Phos., Sulph.
- Mal-assimination: Abrot., Calc., China, Iod., Nat-m., Sil.
- Mental remedies: Anac., Bell., Hyos., Stram.
- Milk non-pregnant: Asaf., Cycl., Merc-sol.
- Nausea – smell of food: Cocc., Coloc., Sep.
- Navel: Calc-p., Mang., Plat., Plb.
- Nightly bone pains: Asaf., Aur., Merc-sol.
- No appetite – no thirst: Ant-c., Ant-t., Hydr., Puls.
- No fever remedies: Camph., Cocc., Coloc., Con., Spong., Stict.

- No inflammation: Cocc., Coloc., Con., Spong., Sticta.

- No relief – belching: Arg-n., China, Lyc.

- Oedema and dropsy: Acet-ac., Apis, Apoc., Ars., China., Dig., Kali-c., Phos.

- Only wind passes: Aloe, Nat-s.

- Orderly state: China., Nat-m.

- Palate itches: Sabad., Wyethia.

- Paralysis – single part: Caust.

- Paralytic weakness during menses: Alum., Carb-an., Cocc-i.

- Patch up remedies: Arn., Ars., Cocc., Lyc., Nux-v., Puls., Rumx., Sang., Senec., Seneg., Stann., Tarent-c.

- Periodic: Ars., Chin., Nat-m.

- Piles: Aesc., Aloe, Coll., Ham., Hyper., Ign., Lach., Lil-t., Mur-ac., Nux-v., Sulph.

- Potatoes make worse: Alum., Coloc.

- Puffed face: Ars., Asaf., Aur-met., Carb-an., Carb-v., Phos., Puls.

- Rapid acting remedies: Acon., Bapt., Bell., Canth., Cham., Coloc.
- Rare type asthma: Ambr., Asaf.
- Rheumatic eye balls: Aesc.
- Rheumatic heart: Aur-met., Cact., Kalm., Led., Rhus-t.
- Rheumatic menses: Cimic.
- Rheumatic stomach: Ant-c.
- Rheumatic teeth: Colch.
- Ring worm – hair: Bacc., Dulc., Thuj.
- Rolls head: Apis, Bell., Podo.
- Saliva – frothy: Lach., Nux-m.
- Saliva profuse: Bar-c., Ip., Lach., Merc., Nat-s.,
- Scalp eruptions: Ars., Calc., Dulc., Graph., Petr., Sep., Sulph.
- Scanty urine or retained: Acon., Apis, Bry., Camph., Canth., Caust., Cupr., Merc-c., Op., Phyt., Plb., Verat.
- Scanty urine: Apis, Ars., Hell., Op., Plb.

- Sickness – lifting: Calc-fl., Graph., Rhus-t.
- Sleeps in chair: Alum., Nux-m., Ph-ac., Sabad.
- Sleepy – always: Nux-m., Op.
- Smells sour: Hep., Nat-p., Rheum.
- Snores: Ant-t., Laur., Op.
- Soft stool: Alum., Chin., Nux-m., Psor.
- Soles burn: Aloe, Cham., Fl-ac.,. Led., Lil-t., Med., Petr., Puls., Sang., Sulph.
- Soles sensitive to walk: Ant-c., Med., Ruta., Sil.
- Spine feels hot: Alum., Lyc., Phos.
- Splinters under nails: Cic., Led., Hyper.
- Spreading ulcers: Ars., Dulc., Merc.
- Stool slips back: Sanic., Sil., Thuj.
- Stringy mucus: Cocc., Hydr., Kali-bi.
- Sun headache: Cact., Kalm., Nat-m., Sang., Stann.
- Syphilitic nose: Asaf., Aur., Hep.
- Testes and mammary glands dwindle: Iod.

- Testes swollen: Aur-m., Clem., Puls., Rhod.
- Thirstless: Apis, Gels., Ip., Nux-m., Puls.
- Throat – sensation splinters: Alum., Arg-n., Hep., Nat-m., Nit-ac.
- Toothache on lying: Cham., Clem., Mag-c.
- Urine spurts with cough: Caust., Nat-m., Puls., Sars., Squil.
- Uvula – swollen: Apis, Kali-bi., Kali-i., Lach., Mur-ac., Nit-ac., Phos.
- Vegetable mercury: Phyt., Podo.
- Vegetable Sulphur: Lyc., Puls.
- Vomiting and purging: Arg-n., Verat.
- Vulva sensitive: Coff., Plat.
- Water gurgles while drinking: Cupr., Phos., Verat.
- Widows – widowers: Apis, Cimic., Con.
- Winter cough: Ars., Dulc., Psor.
- Worms: Cina, Graph., Nat-p., Sabad., Sep., Sil., Sin-n.

- Worse – warmth: Apis, Guaj., Lac-c., Led., Puls., Sec.

- Worse coition: Ambr., Asaf., Kali-c.

- Worse fast: Anac., Cist., Iod., Lyc.

- Worse Ice cream: Ars., Nat-s., Puls.

- Worse motion: Bell., Bry., Cad-s., Cocc., Colch.

- Worse water: Bell., Canth., Hyos., Stram.

- Worse winter: Cist., Petr.

Remarks: Kent concises and consolidates many things; and this gives us a treasure which we may use when we find suitable. Above are only few collections from Kent's vast ocean. **A few of these may be from *else where also.***

The readers may build their own structure by adding or changing where ever they so feel or like. But this should give them a basis to study Kent better and more thoroughly.

12

KENT AND DEEPER MODALITIES

We find in *Kent's* Lectures a mention of some deeper modalities - which we do not commonly find in other works. Some of these are given below:

ARSENIC ALB.

- Therefore, we say a striking feature belonging to this medicine is relief of all complaints of the body from wrapping up and from warmth in general, and relief of the complaints of the head by cold, *except the external complaints of the head, which are better from heat and from wrapping up. The neuralgias of the face and eyes, and above the eyes are better from heat.*

- We know that in acute conditions of Arsenic, there is either thirst for ice cold, water, and for only enough to moisten the mouth or there is thirst for water in large quantities and yet it does not quench the thirst, but this thirsty stage goes on to another in which there is aversion to water and hence we see that in chronic diseases, Arsenic is thirstless.

- A peculiar feature of the thirst is that there is no thirst during the *chill* except for hot drinks; during the *heat* there is thirst little and often for water enough to moisten the mouth, which is almost no thirst, and during the *sweat* there is thirst for large drinks.

BELLADONNA

- The complaints of Bell. in a general way are ameliorated from rest, and aggravated from motion; but there is a kind of restlessness with tearing pain from hips down, most trouble some to observe, that keeps the patient walking all the time.

- Bell. is full if thirst, we find when we come to study the stomach symptoms. Some times Bell. wants large quantities, some times water constantly to wet the mouth, like Ars.

BRYONIA

- It is common for Bry. to be ameliorated from cool air, and from cool applications. Now, if he moves, he gets warmed up, the pains are worse, *but there are rheumatic complaints of Bry. which are better from heat and under these circumstances, he is better from continued motion. It is another form of relief, and another of the modalities.*

- Most of the head complaints that are of congestive character are better from cool applications, from cold air, etc. *Yet there are some of the Bry. head complaints that are relieved by hot applications,* and these seem to have no accompanying cerebral congestion. So that **Bry. has opposite modalities,** but in all its opposite states, there is still a grand nature running all through, sufficient to detect it.

- It is very *common* for the Bry. patient to have great thirst; he is apt to drink large quantities of water, at wide intervals. With this dry, brown tongue, however, he losses his taste for water and does not want it; dry mouth and thirstless like *Nux-m.*

- Stomach complaints of Bry. are relieved from

warm drinks; that becomes a particular because his desire is for cold drinks, but his *stomach is better from warm drinks.*

- Sensitiveness of the pit of the stomach and sensitiveness over the whole abdomen. This is commonly *relieved by heat, although the patient himself wants to lie in a cold room.* The heat of the room is oppressive, **yet heat applied is agreeable.**

- *Whole stomach and abdomen - sensitive to pressure.*

The great homeopathic scholar Catherine R. Coulter says, **"There are no absolutes in homeopathy.** A Silica patient need not be chilly, a Sep. one can sparkle with cheerfulness and mirth, Nat-m. can dislike salt. Arsenic may be unconcerned about his health."

The above few examples are just to point out that our studies have to be wide and deep so that we can understand the various situations and deal with them successfully.

13

KENT – THE SHADOW SIDE

ABOUT TUBERCULINUM

I do not use Tub. merely because it is a nosode, or with the idea that generally prevails of using nosodes; that, a product of the disease for the disease, and the results of the disease. This I fear is too much with the prevailing thought in using nosodes. In certain places it prevails and is taught that anything relating to Syphilis must be treated with *Syph.*; that anything relating to Gonorrhea, must be treated with *Med.*, anything Psoric must be treated with *Psor.*, and any thing that relates to Tuberculosis must be treated with Tub.

That will go out of use some day; it is more isopathy; and it is an *unsound doctrine*. It is not the better idea of homeopathy. It is not based upon sound principles. **It belongs to a hysterical homeopathy that prevails in the century.**

Yet much good has come out of it.

Comments: We all know that the four 'nosodes' – most important of all, are playing a *vital role* in treating difficult cases in homeopathy. We also know that these nosodes are drugs in 'potency' irrespective of what they are and that they derive their origin from disease products.

Then *Dr. Kent admits* that much good has come out of them.

He further says, "It is hoped that *provings may be made* so that we may be able to prescribe Tub. on the symptoms of Tub. just as we would use any drug.

But this requires a reference to what he says in the concluding lines of Gels. chapter. "Though Gels. *may not have produced Erysipelas* it will stop the progress of the disease in a *few hours* and the patient will go to a quick recovery. Again, "If we master thoroughly the materia medica, we do not stop to see if a remedy produces certain kinds of inflammation, etc. but we **consider the *state of the patient.*"**

In such situation, the use of the nosodes is never *hysterical*. If we strictly go to provings, **we have very few remedies that can be said as "well proved".** Most of our remedies are either partly proved or their provings are not reliable.

Dr. J.C. Burnett has brought - such aspects of Bac. and Med. to light that may not be possible even after process of *'proving'*. Many qualities of Thuja also are made known to us by his **own method or clinical testimony – which would have remained unknown inspite of provings conducted.**

The great *scholar Catherine R. Coulter* finds that *"Hahnemann himself never refined completely,* the concept of the miasm or resolved the conflict inherent in attempting to classify diseases according to their miasmatic origin, and the homeopathic stress on the totality of the symptoms together with the necessity of individualizing. *This has left room for others to step in and fill the doctrinal* void with theories."

She further says, "While the miasmic theory may at times explain the origin and development of the patients illness, it is not a technique for finding the patient's remedy (whether nosode or other.)"

In the above circumstances, we have no other way than to *accept the truth* that our 'pathy' is still in 'adolescence' and many more *explorations* are required to make it a '*developed science.*'

The remarks of Dr. Kent here are similar to Dr. J.C. Burnett who called '*Surgeons*' as '*Carpentors*' and eye surgeons as mere '*mechanics*'. We should know that we are on way to *achievements* and the ultimate goal is *far far away.*

Dr. Kent himself remarked in his chapter of Lac. can. that it may take a '*Century*' to prove this drug to our satisfaction, and we cannot ignore and overlook the *hard reality* that 'provings' earlier conducted during the life of Dr. Hahnemann, Hering and some others cannot be expected in near future. It requires dedication by *educated healthy persons* of different sex and from different regions to take up this task.

The people today merely want a thing, they simply desire, they only *wish* certain things to be done – but **not at their cost.**

"Khwab to ye hain ki hum asman ki sair Karen.

Hausala ye hai ki Parwaz se ghabrate hain."

(We always wish to take journey to the sky; but the fact is that we do not gather the courage to take a flight.)

Dr. Kent was a great genius and his contributions are so great that we may lack adequate words to express; still no body is perfect and some times his shadow side expresses itself. This has been simply mentioned because the study of the great pioneer would not have been balanced in the absence of this discussion.

HOMEOPATHY – IN ONE WORD

If we concise the definition of homeopathy, the only word which can *contain* it to the greatest extent is *simillimum*. Homeopathy has to be in and around *simillimum*. If it is not so, it is not homeopathy - it is anything else !

14

HOMEOPATHY NEEDS ONE MORE KENT

Kents as we have seen from his literature was very conscientious, truthful and a devoted homeopath. He could not tolerate the idea that people use the 'nosodes' on a large scale without their 'provings'. He called such practice as *'hysterical homeopathy.'*

But things have gone too worse since then. About *Tub.*, it is told that different 'pioneers' have been using it differently e.g. **One way** of using it was to give a dose and then *repeat* it after six months. That is all. **Another extreme** was to give twelve doses in a day *and continue this for 10 days.* In between these extremes, three more types developed for giving this *'nosode.'*

This is really more '*hysterical*' a way to differ to such an extent in repeating such an important remedy. Actually, many aspects of homeopathy need a careful examination and a balanced and agreed approach for the millions of practitioners who are confused every now and then over such issues.

It is true that a subject like 'homeopathy' has to be treated differently from other 'pathies' as it cannot be too rigid in its application or use. Individual preferences are more needed here than in other 'pathies'. But the **flexibility** should not go to the extent of eccentricity which even **apparently** confuses the common practitioners.

Dr. Kent has always been balanced in his approaches. He cautioned us where we are required to be careful, and guided us for such occasions where we want quick and safe results. His pointing to the surface or patch-up remedies is very glaring example of this.

When he warns us against use of *Ferrum* or *Sulph.* for morning diarrhea of the consumptives, he advises us to use *Rumex* which is safe for such conditions. "*Rumex* is one of the most valuable palliatives in advanced phthisis; it will often carry a case through another winter" For Ferrum, he says, "*Ferrum* will stop the diarrhea, but the patient will not live long."

He always warns us against unsafe conditions, unsafe remedies, unsafe diets with certain remedies, cautious use of certain remedies in certain states etc. People in general – have been given an impression that Homeopathy is *safe and always safe*. So they take it in that way. *Even* common practitioners think like this when they do not study the literature in detail and deeply.

It is *Kent* who makes us conscious of all this. His '*lectures*' contain almost all aspects of practice and use of medicine.

We need an another Kent to speak on various matters which still remain unsettled – boldly, clearly, selflessly, and conscientiously.

Catherine R. Coulter, the bold scholar of the present age – says, **"Seldom will a remedy cover the totality of symptoms for all time."** Then **"There are no absolutes in homeopathy."** A *Silicea* patient need not be chilly, a *Sep.* one can sparkle with cheerfulness and mirth. *Nat-m.* can dislike salt, *Arsenic* may be quite unconcerned about his health and *Puls.* can be full of thirst.: *And suggests in this context that,* **"To remain vital and meaningful, the homeopathic materia medica, like any aspect of our cultural heritage, must be repeatedly scrutinized, analyzed, and interpreted by each generation in the light of its new knowledge and understanding."**

And such ideas once more make us remember *Kent* who told everything fearlessly – even accepted his shortcomings without hesitation!

NATRIUM MUR.

A child died of snake bite. The members of the family were sad. The child was to be taken for burial. A neighbouring old woman came thee. She asked – where did the snake bite the child? Child's mother replied – it was below the eye. The old woman said, "It is very kind of God. *The eye was saved!"*

It is like Nat-m. The man does not or cannot keep care of the significance of what he speaks. *He slips, when he speaks.*

15

PERSONIFICATION – IN HOMEOPATHY

Previously it was the sphere of literature to establish a simile to present a vivid picture of an idea or an object or a scene. It was a part of this aim to personify an inanimate object and create a fervour in the presentation. The 'Epics' and 'Poetry' especially constituted this phenomenon.

But it was *homeopathy* to create individualities and personify drugs in the field of medicine, and that too with *living human characters,* and still more very authentically on the *basis of proving* of the drugs on healthy human beings. It has been a feat of medical science not only to imagine, but to explore and establish that objects of *'Nature'* – whether *animal*, *vegetable*, or *metal* – simply dorment or outwardly active in crude form – *contain a lively* or terrible or simple, or a very deeply complicated personality *'when potentized'* – to represent all the physical, mental and emotional traits of a man – subject to identification and verification when so required.

HOMEOPATHIC

Whatever we purchase from a homeopathic shop, we call it homeopathic, whatever we take from a homeopathic physician, we call it homeopathic. But homeopathic remedy is only that which is based on 'simillimum' and nothing except and beyond that.

16

COMPLEMENTARIES AND INIMICALS AT A GLANCE

(Only those in common use)

COMPLEMENTARIES

Acetic acid	: Chin.
Acidum fluor.	: Sil.
Acidum nit.	: Ars., Thuj.
Acid sulph.	: Puls.
Acid mur.	: Bry., Rhus-t.
Aconite	: Arn., Coff., Sulph.
Aethusa	: Calc.
Allium cepa	: Phos., Puls., Sars., Thuj.

Alum	: Bry., Ferr.
Aloe	: Sulph.
Antimonium tart.	: Bar-c., Bry.
Apis mel.	: Nat-m.
Arnica mon.	: Acon., Bry., Hyper., Ip., Rhus-t., Spig., Verat.,
Arsenicum alb.	: All-s., Carb-v., Nat-s., Phos., Pyrog., Thuj.
Badiaga	: Iod., Merc-s., Sulph.
Baryta carb.	: Dulc., Psor.
Belladonna	: Calc., Cham.
Bryonia	: Alum., Mur-ac., Phyt., Rhus-t., Sulph.
Calcarea carb.	: Bell., Lyc., Rhus-t., Sil.
Calcarea phos.	: Ruta.
Calendula	: Hep.
Camphor	: Canth.
Carbo-an.	: Calc-p.
Carbo-v.	: Ars., Dros., Kali-c., Phos.,
Causticum	: Carb-v., Coloc., Petros.
Chamomilla	: Bell., Mag-c.

China	: Ars., Carb-v., Ferr.
Coffea	: Acon.
Conium mac.	: Bar-m.
Cuprum	: Ars., Calc., Sulph.
Drosera	: Bar-c., Carb-v., Cina, Kali-s., Nux-v., Sulph.
Ferrum	: Alum., Chin., Ham.
Graphites	: Arg-n., Ars., Caust., Ferr-m., Hep., Lyc., Tub.
Hamamelis	: Ferr.
Hepar sulph.	: Calend.
Ignatia	: Nat-m.
Iodium	: Lyc.
Ipecacuanha	: Ant-t., Arn., Cupr.
Kalium carb.	: Carb-v., Nux-v.
Kalmia lat..	: Benz-ac., Gels., Spig.
Lachesis	: Hep., Lyc.
Lycopodium	: Iod., Hydr., Lach., Puls.
Magnesium carb.	: Cham.
Mercurius sol.	: Bad., Sulph.

Natrium mur.	: Apis, Ign., Sep.
Natrium sulph.	: Ars., Thuj.
Nux-vom.	: Sep., Kali-c., Sulph.
Palladium	: Plat.
Phosphorus	: All-c., Ars., Carb-v., Tub.
Psorinum	: Sulph., Tub.
Pulsatilla	: All-c., Kali-c., Kali-m., Lyc., Sil., Sul-ac.
Rhus-tox.	: Bry., Calc., Mur-ac., Phyt.
Rumex	: Calc.
Sabadilla.	: Sep.
Sabina.	: Psor., Thuj.
Sarsaparilla	: All-c., Merc., Sep.
Sepia.	: Nat-m., Nux-v., Sabad., Sulph.
Silicea	: Fl-ac., Calc., Puls., Sanic., Thuj.,
Stannum met.	: Puls.
Staphysagria	: Caust., Coloc.
Sulphur	: Acon., Aloe, Ars., Bad., Bry., Calc., Carb-v., Graph., Nux-v., Psor., Sars., Sep., Sil.

Thuja occ.	: Ars., Bac., Med., Nat-s., Sabin., Sil.
Tuberculinum	: Bar-c., Bell., Calc., Hydr., Psor., Sulph.
Veratatrum alb.	: Arn., Ars., Cupr.

INIMICALS

Aceticum acid	: Bell., Borx., Caust., Nux-v., Ran-b., Sars.
Acid nitricum	: Calc., Lach.
Allium cep.	: All-s., Aloe, Squil.
Allium sat.	: All-c., Aloe, Squil.
Ammonium carb.	: Lach.
Apis mel.	: Rhus-t.
Aurum mur. nat.	: Coff.
Baryta carb.	: Calc.
Belladonna.	: Acet-ac., Dulc.
Borax.	: Acet-ac.
Bovinum.	: Coff.
Bryonia	: Sep.
Calcarea carb.	: Bar-c., Kali-bi., Nit-ac., Sulph.

Cantharis	: Coff.
Carbo an.	: Carb-v.
Carbo veg.	: Carb-an., Kreos.
Caulophyllum.	: Coff.
Causticum	: Acet-ac., Coff., Phos.
Chamomilla.	: Zinc-m.
China off.	: Dig., Sel.
Cistus can.	: Coff.
Cocc.	: Coff.
Coffea	: Aur-m-n., Canth., Caul., Caust., Cist., Cocc., Ign., Lyc., Mill., Stram.
Digitalinum	: Chin.
Dulcamara	: Acet-ac., Bell., Lach.
Ferrum met.	: Acet-ac.
Ignatia	: Coff., Nux-v.,
Kalium bich.	: Calc.
Kreosote	: Carb-v.
Lachesis	: Acet-ac., Amm-c., Dulc., Nit-ac., Psor.
Ledum pal.	: Chin.

Lycopodium	: Calc., Coff.
Mercurius sol.	: Acet-ac., Sil.
Millefolium	: Coff.
Nux vom.	: Acet-ac., Ign., Zinc.
Phosphorus	: Caust.
Psorinum	: Sep.
Pulsatilla.	: Sep.
Ranunculus bulb.	: Acet-ac., Staph., Sulph.
Rhus-tox.	: Apis.
Sarsaparilla	: Acet-ac.
Selenium.	: Chin.
Sepia	: Bry., Lach., Puls.
Silicea	: Merc-s.
Scilla mar.	: All-c., All-s.
Staphysagria.	: Ran-b.

STUDY OF MAN

Man cannot be seen and understood in fragments. We can study him as a whole – not only physically, but also mentally and emotionally. *And it is homeopathy* which considers man with all aspects.

17

ARSENICUM ALBUM

A father said to his son, "Son, I want to see you very prosperous – so that people say – here is the *worthy son* of a worthy father."

The son said, "Oh. No dady. I want to touch heights where people say - You *are the father* of such worthy person."

And this is Arsenic.

* **Arsenic alb.**

Arsenic is like a horse and the horses are of *three types.* So Arsenic presents three types of personalities.

- **The race horse:** Very nervous, very sensitive, fast, ready to run, wants to supercede.

- **The farm horse:** Eating, resting, fastidious, attended well, getting along someone comfortably.

- **The cart horse:** Like wood pecker — drilling non-stop. Without appearing to tire. Does not sweat.

And Arsenic has the widest range to influence man.

FOUR DIMENSIONS

Kent advised us to keep four dimensions in mind with using homeopathic remedies; the sphere of the remedy, the state of the patient and the medicine, relating to that state, the stage of the disease and the medicine suitable to that stage and then the connecting symptoms. If we miss one factor to consider, we shall fail to find a perfect 'simillimum.'

18

WE EXPECT

In Homeopathy, we expect everything to have been done by *Hahnemann*; we expect everything to have been told by Hahnemann! We study the science from this angle, we practice the science with this angle!

We do not take into consideration, the advancements made in the *general science.* "Now we know that time is not absolute as thought in the 19th century, but it shortens, lengthens and even stands still near a Black Hole. In the last century, we did not know about atomic structure, about X-rays, lasers, radio waves, super conductivity, rockets, computers, nuclear energy, Xerox machines, telex, fax, about why the Sun shines, about Pulsars, quasars and so on. Within a century, we have come far off."

Homeopathy of 19th century developed as a system, emerged as a science. But "Science" in the words of Dr. M.L. Tyler "means knowledge," and it has to develop every moment.

We have so far come to know that '*Potencies*' work, they exhibit the faculties of mind also. Importance of '*simillimum*' has been established, but only *few* drugs have been *explored* so far.

When we study homeopathy – we must be *scientific* in our attitude, and not *religious* to follow it with simple faith. It is then that we can achieve the dream of the great scientist Hahnemann who wished to see homeopathy – *"the mathematical science in certainty."*

WE DO NOT GO DEEP

Dr. Kent says about **Nux. vom.** "It is given as a **routine** remedy for loss of appetite. It will increase the appetite but do **dangerous** work to the patient." We take things lightly always and do not study homeopathic principles as to how the same drug does **immense good** and also prove **dangerous when** we rightly used.

19

WHEN I AM GONE!

Lord Jesus told, *'As long as* I am in the world, I am the light of the world, and when I am gone, the light is gone.'

This is true with all incarnations. When they have gone, the *ideals* have left with them, the **followers have simply fought for them, and never lived for them.**

Lord Krishna fought for justice, he struggled for goodness to prevail upon evils, but after he left – every thing came to a stand still. The bravery of 'Arjuna' could not work against few robbers.

Lord Ram sacrificed in all aspects of his life. He was a deity of dedication. But people who followed him were all selfish and greedy – they remember him

– lest he could free them with fear – during and after this life.

The great Socrates took the deadly *poison* without hesitation for the *Truth* he told. His *ugly* wife poured hot water on him when he addressed his audience. People asked, "How do you tolerate this lady who is so ugly both at body and mind." He smilingly told, "It is she who has taught me tolerance." And how many have learnt the *virtues* for which he lived and dedicated his life!

Hahnemann originated homeopathy as a science. He dreamed to make it "the mathematical science in certainty." The followers have to see what they have done to fulfill his dream!

CAMOUFLAGING SYMPTOMS

We sometimes thicki that if some symptoms are removed or they are changed, a cure has taken place. Dr. Kent has warned us mask, the symptoms, and fail to cure, He says, "The homoeopathic failures are the worst failures on earth.

20

CASE AND ACTION

Non-violence is related to action, *Love* is related to cause. If there is no love, the word non-violence is meaningless.

The slogan of non-violence in the present age is artificial and so ineffective.

You cannot see your *beloved* or loving child into distress. A drop of tear is enough to *upset* you. But where ever you are not bound by love, the death of a million people will not *move* your heart. You may speak about it – but will not weep on it.

Love is engendered by understanding and emotion, and it establishes peace and pleasure. Any action on intellectual level is superficial and bears no fruit.

Jesus was full of love, *Buddha* was sparkling with love, *Mahavir* was fountain of love, *Kabir* was ocean of love and so were all our incarnations and saints. It is therefore that they could fill the atmosphere with fragrance of *Love Devine.* **The so-called followers are *labeled bottles* without wine, and we cannot expect *more than slogans* from them.**

Homeopathy today is *expanding* in followings, but the spirit of *exploration* is dwindling, because it needs dedication to explore, and it requires *real love* to dedicate.

WHEN ARSENIC NOT RESTLESS!

"As **uneasiness** comes in the **early stage** of disease, and lasts but until the prostration becomes marked. While lying in bed, at first be moves his whole body, moves himself in bed and out of bed, but the prostration becomes so marked that he is able to move only his limbs until atlast he becomes so weak that he is no longer able to move and he lies in perfect quiet in extreme prostration. It seems that **prostration takes** the place of anxiety and restlessness, and he appears like a cadaver."

Dr. Kent

21

FEAR, FAITH AND LOVE

Mankind has been attributed by Nature with three things especially – Fear, Faith and Love.

Fear is the greatest curse which hovers around man. It is embedded in his life and imagination. Man fears for his present, fears in anticipation from future, fears from death, and fears from hell in the next birth.

Faith counteracts fear to a great extent. Man takes shelter in faith when fearful. He has created hundreds and thousands of deities to pin his faith and to bank upon when in fear, although the *Real Entity* is one and only one for all and for all times. Faith makes his life tolerable to some extent. He is tortured the most **when his faith is shaken or hurt or is in crisis.**

Love is the highest bliss for man. It is divinely bestowed upon man. The love of worldly objects is all surrounded by fear. Where ever there is worldly love, there is fear! But the *Love Devine* is free from fear.

Realization of self is the ladder to Love Devine.

Homeopathy affects the physical, mental and emotional aspects of man. Consequently, it influences his inner self. *It lessens fear, strengthens faith and modifies perverted love.* **It prepares the man to see the benign Nature at work through the realm of medicines,** where an inert substance turns into a living and vibrating creation – when potentized, identical to man in feelings and emotions!

HOMEOPATHY!

Somebody asked his friend - how to recognise a homeopath! The reply was - "He who boasts of curing all incurables e.g. cancer, AIDS, and so on, is sure a homeopath of first order!

SYMPTOMS AND SPHERES

The study of *Symptoms* and *Spheres* of medicines – both are equally important in homeopathy. Who can question the powers of *Aconite* to release the tension of arteries, of *Arnica* to tone up the walls of blood vessels, of *Chamomilla* to soothe the turmoil of mind. of *Hypericum* to repair and soothe the nerve centres, of *Cactus* to regularize the circulation; and many more such drugs where we **cannot ignore the spheres at the cost of some insignificant symptoms.**

Symptoms are essentially to be studied as a rule, but great care is needed to bank upon them – because they may be partially proved, or over proved, or only regionally proved, or unscientifically proved, or not well recorded!

There are millions and millions of such drugs which are yet to be derived from various Kingdoms (i.e. Plants, animals and metals) and put to process of provings and to be studied with regard to their symptoms and spheres.

BOOKS BY THE SAME AUTHOR

- The Homeopathic Physicians's Quick Prescriber, 2nd Edition
- Homeopathic Chalisa, Hindi, 2nd Edition
- Rasoi Chalisa, Hindi, 2nd Edition
- 250 years of Homeopathy, 2nd Edition
- Secrets of Sure and Quick Results, 2nd Edition
- Some Essential References in Repertory, 2nd Edition
- Augmented Supplement of Dr. W. Boericke's Materia Medica, 2nd Edition
- The Concepts of Miasms in Homeopathy and New Era, 2nd Edition
- A Concise Materia Medica of Mental Symptoms, 2nd Edition
- A Table Talk in Homeopathy, 2nd Edition
- Look Busy do Nothing, Hindi, 2nd Edition
- Wonders of a Single Dose in Homeopathy, 2nd Edition
- Life Saving Drugs in Homeopathy
- Advanced Homeopathy
- Quick Prescriber in Homeopathy
- Drug Zones in Homeopathy